W9-CBV-564

CROCK·POT
◆ THE ORIGINAL SLOW COOKER ◆

Recipes

Publications International, Ltd.

Pictured on the front cover: Easy Beef Stew *(page 62).*

Pictured on the back cover *(left to right):* Overnight Breakfast Porridge *(page 10),* Chicken and Vegetable Soup *(page 54)* and Sausage and Peppers over Polenta *(page 92).*

ISBN: 978-1-68022-137-4

Library of Congress Control Number: 201593886

Manufactured in China.

8 7 6 5 4 3 2 1

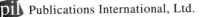 Publications International, Ltd.

Table of Contents

Slow Cooking Tips 4

Breakfast Favorites 8

Meatless Monday 30

Soups, Stews and Chilies 54

Meaty Main Dishes 78

Sensational Sides 102

Page 8   Page 106   Page 90

Sizes of CROCK-POT® Slow Cookers

Smaller **CROCK-POT®** slow cookers—such as 1- to 3½-quart models—are the perfect size for cooking for singles, a couple or empty nesters (and also for serving dips).

While medium-size **CROCK-POT®** slow cookers (those holding somewhere between 3 quarts and 5 quarts) will easily cook enough food to feed a small family. They are also convenient for holiday side dishes or appetizers.

Large **CROCK-POT®** slow cookers are great for large family dinners, holiday entertaining and potluck suppers. A 6- to 7-quart model is ideal if you like to make meals in advance, or have dinner tonight and store leftovers for another day.

Types of CROCK-POT® Slow Cookers

Current **CROCK-POT®** slow cookers come equipped with many different features and benefits, from auto cook programs to oven-safe stoneware to timed programming. Please visit **WWW.CROCK-POT.COM** to find the **CROCK-POT®** slow cooker that best suits your needs.

How you plan to use a **CROCK-POT®** slow cooker may affect the model you choose to purchase. For everyday cooking, choose a size large enough to serve your family. If you plan to use the **CROCK-POT®** slow cooker primarily for entertaining, choose one of the larger sizes. Basic **CROCK-POT®** slow cookers can hold as little as 16 ounces or as much as 7 quarts. The smallest sizes are great for keeping dips warm on a buffet, while the larger sizes can more readily fit large quantities of food and larger roasts.

Cooking, Stirring and Food Safety

CROCK-POT® slow cookers are safe to leave unattended. The outer heating base may get hot as it cooks, but it should not pose a fire hazard. The heating element in the heating base functions at a low wattage and is safe for your countertops.

Your **CROCK-POT®** slow cooker should be filled about one-half to three-fourths full for most recipes unless otherwise instructed. Lean meats such as chicken or pork tenderloin will cook faster than meats with more connective tissue and fat such as beef chuck or pork shoulder. Bone-in meats will take longer than boneless cuts. Typical **CROCK-POT**® slow cooker dishes take approximately 7 to 8 hours to reach the simmer point on LOW and about 3 to 4 hours on HIGH. Once the vegetables and meat start to simmer and braise, their flavors will fully blend and meat will become fall-off-the-bone tender.

According to the U.S. Department of Agriculture, all bacteria are killed at a temperature of 165°F. It's important to follow the recommended cooking times and not open the lid often, especially early in the cooking process when heat is building up inside the unit. If you need to open the lid to check on your food or are adding additional ingredients, remember to allow additional cooking time if necessary to ensure food is cooked through and tender.

Large **CROCK-POT**® slow cookers, the 6- to 7-quart sizes, may benefit from a quick stir halfway through cook time to help distribute heat and promote even cooking. It's usually unnecessary to stir at all, as even ½ cup liquid will help to distribute heat and the stoneware is the perfect medium for holding food at an even temperature throughout the cooking process.

Oven-Safe Stoneware

All **CROCK-POT**® slow cooker removable stoneware inserts may (without their lids) be used safely in ovens at up to 400°F. In addition, all **CROCK-POT**® slow cookers are microwavable without their lids. If you own another slow cooker brand, please refer to your owner's manual for specific stoneware cooking medium tolerances.

Frozen Food

Frozen food can be successfully cooked in a **CROCK-POT**® slow cooker. However, it will require longer cooking time than the same recipe made with fresh food. It is almost always preferable to thaw frozen food prior to placing it in the **CROCK-POT**® slow cooker. Using an instant-read thermometer is recommended to ensure meat is fully cooked through.

Pasta and Rice

If you are converting a recipe for a **CROCK-POT**® slow cooker that calls for uncooked pasta, first cook the pasta on the stovetop just until slightly tender. Then add the pasta to the **CROCK-POT**® slow cooker. If you are converting a recipe for the **CROCK-POT**® slow cooker that calls for cooked rice, stir in raw rice with the other recipe ingredients plus ¼ cup extra liquid per ¼ cup of raw rice.

Beans

Beans must be softened completely before combining with sugar and/or acidic foods in the **CROCK-POT®** slow cooker. Sugar and acid have a hardening effect on beans and will prevent softening. Fully cooked canned beans may be used as a substitute for dried beans.

Vegetables

Root vegetables often cook more slowly than meat. Cut vegetables accordingly to cook at the same rate as meat—large or small or lean versus marbled—and place near the sides or bottom of the stoneware to facilitate cooking.

Herbs

Fresh herbs add flavor and color when added at the end of the cooking cycle; if added at the beginning, many fresh herbs' flavor will dissipate over long cook times. Ground and/or dried herbs and spices work well in slow cooking and may be added at the beginning of the cook time. For dishes with shorter cook times, hearty fresh herbs such as rosemary and thyme hold up well. The flavor power of all herbs and spices can vary greatly depending on their particular strength and shelf life. Use chili powders and garlic powder sparingly, as these can sometimes intensify over the long cook times. Always taste the finished dish and correct seasonings including salt and pepper.

Liquids

It's not necessary to use more than ½ to 1 cup liquid in most instances since juices in meats and vegetables are retained more in slow cooking than in conventional cooking. Excess liquid can be cooked down and concentrated after slow cooking on the stovetop or by removing meat and vegetables from stoneware, stirring in one of the following thickeners and setting the **CROCK-POT®** slow cooker to HIGH. Cover; cook on HIGH for approximately 15 minutes or until juices are thickened.

FLOUR: All-purpose flour is often used to thicken soups or stews. Stir cold water into the flour in a small bowl until smooth. With the **CROCK-POT®** slow cooker on HIGH, whisk the flour mixture into the liquid in the **CROCK-POT®** slow cooker. Cover; cook on HIGH 15 minutes or until the mixture is thickened.

CORNSTARCH: Cornstarch gives sauces a clear, shiny appearance; it's used most often for sweet dessert sauces and stir-fry sauces. Stir cold water into the cornstarch in a small bowl until the cornstarch dissolves. Quickly stir this mixture into the liquid in the **CROCK-POT®** slow cooker; the sauce will thicken as soon as the liquid simmers. Cornstarch breaks down with too much heat, so never add it at the beginning of the slow cooking process and turn off the heat as soon as the sauce thickens.

ARROWROOT: Arrowroot (or arrowroot flour) comes from the root of a tropical plant that is dried and ground to a powder; it produces a thick, clear sauce. Those who are allergic to wheat often use it in place of flour. Place arrowroot in a small bowl or cup and stir in cold water until the mixture is smooth. Quickly stir this mixture into the liquid in the **CROCK-POT®** slow cooker. Arrowroot thickens below the boiling point, so it even works well in a **CROCK-POT®** slow cooker on LOW. Too much stirring can break down an arrowroot mixture.

TAPIOCA: Tapioca is a starchy substance extracted from the root of the cassava plant. Its greatest advantage is that it withstands long cooking, making it an ideal choice for slow cooking. Add it at the beginning of cooking and you'll get a clear thickened sauce in the finished dish. Dishes using tapioca as a thickener are best cooked on the LOW setting; tapioca may become stringy when boiled for a long time.

Milk

Milk, cream and sour cream break down during extended cooking. When possible, add them during the last 15 to 30 minutes of slow cooking, until just heated through. Condensed soups may be substituted for milk and may cook for extended times.

Fish

Fish is delicate and should be stirred into the **CROCK-POT®** slow cooker gently during the last 15 to 30 minutes of cooking time. Cover and cook just until cooked through and serve immediately.

Baked Goods

If you wish to prepare bread, cakes or pudding cakes in a **CROCK-POT®** slow cooker, you may want to purchase a covered, vented metal cake pan accessory for your **CROCK-POT®** slow cooker. You can also use any straight-sided soufflé dish or deep cake pan that will fit into the stoneware of your unit. Baked goods can be prepared directly in the stoneware; however, they can be a little difficult to remove from the insert, so follow the recipe directions carefully.

Maple, Bacon and Raspberry Pancake

Makes 4 servings

5 slices bacon

2 cups pancake mix

1 cup water

½ cup maple syrup, plus additional for serving

1 cup fresh raspberries

3 tablespoons chopped pecans, toasted*

*To toast pecans, spread in single layer in heavy skillet. Cook over medium heat 1 to 2 minutes or until nuts are lightly browned, stirring frequently.

1. Heat large skillet over medium heat. Add bacon; cook 7 to 8 minutes or until crisp. Remove to paper-towel lined plate; crumble.

2. Brush inside of 4- to 5-quart **CROCK-POT**® slow cooker with 1 to 2 tablespoons bacon fat from skillet. Combine pancake mix, water and ½ cup syrup in large bowl; stir to blend. Pour half of batter into **CROCK-POT**® slow cooker; top with half of raspberries, half of bacon and half of pecans. Pour remaining half of batter over top; sprinkle with remaining raspberries, bacon and pecans.

3. Cover; cook on HIGH 1½ to 2 hours or until pancake has risen and is cooked through. Turn off heat. Let stand, uncovered, 10 to 15 minutes. Remove pancake from **CROCK-POT**® slow cooker; cut into eight pieces. Serve with additional syrup.

Overnight Breakfast Porridge

Makes 4 servings

¾ cup steel-cut oats

¼ cup quinoa, rinsed and drained

¼ cup dried cranberries, plus
 additional for serving

¼ cup raisins

3 tablespoons ground flax seeds

2 tablespoons chia seeds

¼ teaspoon cinnamon

2½ cups almond milk, plus additional
 for serving

Maple syrup

¼ cup sliced almonds, toasted*

**To toast almonds, spread in single layer in
heavy skillet. Cook over medium heat 1 to
2 minutes or until nuts are lightly browned,
stirring frequently.*

1. Combine oats, quinoa, ¼ cup cranberries, raisins, flax seeds, chia seeds and cinnamon in a heat-safe bowl that fits inside a 5- or 6-quart **CROCK-POT®** slow cooker. Stir in 2½ cups almond milk.

2. Place bowl in **CROCK-POT®** slow cooker; pour enough water to come halfway up side of bowl.

3. Cover; cook on LOW 8 hours. Carefully remove bowl from **CROCK-POT®** slow cooker. Stir in additional almond milk. Top with syrup, almonds and additional cranberries.

Wake-Up Potato and Sausage Breakfast Casserole

Makes 8 servings

1 pound kielbasa or smoked sausage, diced

1 cup chopped onion

1 cup chopped red bell pepper

1 package (20 ounces) refrigerated Southwestern-style hash browns*

10 eggs

1 cup milk

1 cup (4 ounces) shredded Monterey Jack or sharp Cheddar cheese

*You may substitute O'Brien potatoes and add ½ teaspoon chile pepper.

1. Coat inside of **CROCK-POT®** slow cooker with nonstick cooking spray. Heat large skillet over medium-high heat. Add sausage and onion; cook and stir 6 to 8 minutes or until sausage is browned. Drain fat. Stir in bell pepper.

2. Place one third of potatoes in **CROCK-POT®** slow cooker. Top with half of sausage mixture. Repeat layers. Spread remaining one third of potatoes evenly on top.

3. Whisk eggs and milk in medium bowl. Pour evenly over potatoes. Cover; cook on LOW 6 to 7 hours.

4. Turn off heat. Sprinkle cheese over casserole; let stand 10 minutes or until cheese is melted. Cut into wedges.

Tip: To remove casserole from **CROCK-POT®** slow cooker, omit step 4. Run a rubber spatula around the edge of casserole, lifting the bottom slightly. Invert onto a plate. Place a serving plate on top and invert again. Sprinkle with the cheese and let stand until cheese is melted. To serve, cut into wedges.

Apple-Cinnamon Breakfast Risotto

Makes 6 servings

¼ cup (½ stick) butter

4 medium Granny Smith apples (about 1½ pounds), peeled, cored and diced into ½-inch cubes

1½ teaspoons ground cinnamon

¼ teaspoon ground allspice

¼ teaspoon salt

1½ cups Arborio rice

½ cup packed dark brown sugar

4 cups unfiltered apple juice, at room temperature*

1 teaspoon vanilla

Optional toppings: dried cranberries, sliced almonds and/or milk

*If unfiltered apple juice is unavailable, use any apple juice.

1. Coat inside of **CROCK-POT®** slow cooker with nonstick cooking spray. Melt butter in large skillet over medium-high heat. Add apples, cinnamon, allspice and salt; cook and stir 3 to 5 minutes or until apples begin to release juices. Remove to **CROCK-POT®** slow cooker.

2. Add rice and stir to coat. Sprinkle brown sugar evenly over top. Add apple juice and vanilla. Cover; cook on HIGH 1½ to 2 hours or until all liquid is absorbed. Ladle risotto into bowls; top with desired toppings.

Tip: Keep the lid on! The **CROCK-POT®** slow cooker can take as long as 30 minutes to regain heat lost after the cover is removed.

Savory Sausage Bread Pudding

Makes 4 to 6 servings

4 eggs

2 cups milk *or* 1 cup *each* half-and-half and milk

¼ teaspoon salt

¼ teaspoon black pepper

¼ teaspoon dried thyme

⅛ teaspoon red pepper flakes

1 package (10 ounces) smoked breakfast sausage links, cut into ½-inch pieces

¾ cup (3 ounces) shredded Cheddar cheese

2 cups day-old bread, cut into ½-inch cubes

1. Beat eggs in large bowl. Stir in milk, salt, black pepper, thyme and red pepper flakes. Add sausage, cheese and bread; press bread into egg mixture. Let stand 10 minutes or until liquid is absorbed.

2. Generously butter 2-quart baking dish that fits inside **CROCK-POT®** slow cooker. Pour sausage mixture into baking dish. Cover dish with buttered foil, butter side down.

3. Pour 1 inch of hot water into **CROCK-POT®** slow cooker. Add baking dish. Cover; cook on LOW 4 to 5 hours or until toothpick inserted into center comes out clean.

Orange Date-Nut Bread

Makes 1 loaf

2 cups unbleached all-purpose flour, plus additional for dusting

½ cup chopped pecans

1 teaspoon baking powder

½ teaspoon baking soda

¼ teaspoon salt

1 cup chopped dates

2 teaspoons dried orange peel

⅔ cup boiling water

¾ cup sugar

1 egg, lightly beaten

2 tablespoons shortening

1 teaspoon vanilla

1. Spray 1-quart soufflé dish with nonstick cooking spray; dust with flour.

2. Combine 2 cups flour, pecans, baking powder, baking soda and salt in medium bowl; stir to blend. Combine dates and orange peel in separate medium bowl; pour boiling water over date mixture. Add sugar, egg, shortening and vanilla to date mixture; stir just until blended.

3. Add flour mixture to date mixture; stir just until blended. Pour batter into prepared dish; place in 5-quart **CROCK-POT®** slow cooker. Cover; cook on HIGH 2½ hours or until edges begin to brown.

4. Remove dish from **CROCK-POT®** slow cooker. Cool on wire rack 10 minutes. Remove bread from dish; cool completely.

Variation: Substitute 1 cup dried cranberries for dates.

Blueberry-Banana Pancakes

Makes 4 to 6 servings

2 cups all-purpose flour

⅓ cup sugar

1 tablespoon baking powder

½ teaspoon baking soda

½ teaspoon salt

½ teaspoon ground cinnamon

1¾ cups milk

2 eggs, lightly beaten

¼ cup (½ stick) unsalted butter, melted

1 teaspoon vanilla

1 cup fresh blueberries

2 small bananas, sliced

Maple syrup

1. Combine flour, sugar, baking powder, baking soda, salt and cinnamon in medium bowl; stir to blend. Combine milk, eggs, butter and vanilla in separate medium bowl; stir to blend. Pour milk mixture into flour mixture; stir until moistened. Gently fold in blueberries until mixed.

2. Coat inside of **CROCK-POT**® slow cooker with nonstick cooking spray. Pour batter into **CROCK-POT**® slow cooker. Cover; cook on HIGH 2 hours or until puffed and toothpick inserted into center comes out clean. Cut into wedges; top with sliced bananas and maple syrup.

Spiced Vanilla Applesauce

Makes 6 cups

5 pounds (about 10 medium) sweet apples (such as Fuji or Gala), peeled and cut into 1-inch pieces

½ cup water

2 teaspoons vanilla

1 teaspoon cinnamon

¼ teaspoon grated nutmeg

¼ teaspoon ground cloves

1. Combine apples, water, vanilla, cinnamon, nutmeg and cloves in **CROCK-POT®** slow cooker; stir to blend. Cover; cook on HIGH 3 to 4 hours or until apples are very tender.

2. Turn off heat. Mash mixture with potato masher to smooth out any large lumps. Let cool completely before serving.

Hash Brown and Sausage Breakfast Casserole

Makes 6 to 8 servings

4 cups frozen southern-style hash browns

3 tablespoons unsalted butter

1 large onion, chopped

8 ounces (about 2 cups) sliced mushrooms

3 cloves garlic, minced

2 precooked apple chicken sausages, cut into 1-inch slices

1 package (10 ounces) frozen chopped spinach, thawed and squeezed dry

8 eggs

1 cup milk

1 teaspoon salt

¼ teaspoon black pepper

1½ cups (6 ounces) shredded sharp Cheddar cheese, divided

1. Coat inside of **CROCK-POT®** slow cooker with nonstick cooking spray. Place hash browns in **CROCK-POT®** slow cooker.

2. Melt butter in large nonstick skillet over medium-high heat. Add onion, mushrooms and garlic; cook 4 to 5 minutes, stirring occasionally. Stir in sausage; cook 2 minutes. Add spinach; cook 2 minutes or until mushrooms are tender. Stir sausage mixture into **CROCK-POT®** slow cooker with hash browns until combined.

3. Combine eggs, milk, salt and pepper in large bowl; mix well. Pour over hash brown mixture in **CROCK-POT®** slow cooker. Top with 1 cup cheese. Cover; cook on LOW 4 to 4½ hours or on HIGH 1½ to 2 hours or until eggs are set. Top with remaining ½ cup cheese. Cut into wedges to serve.

Raisin-Oat Quick Bread

Makes 1 loaf

1½ cups all-purpose flour, plus additional for dusting

⅔ cup old-fashioned oats

⅓ cup milk

4 teaspoons baking powder

1 teaspoon ground cinnamon

½ teaspoon salt

½ cup packed raisins

1 cup sugar

2 eggs, slightly beaten

½ cup (1 stick) unsalted butter, melted, plus additional for serving

1 teaspoon vanilla

1. Spray inside of ovenproof glass or ceramic loaf pan that fits inside **CROCK-POT®** slow cooker with nonstick cooking spray; dust with flour.

2. Combine oats and milk in small bowl; let stand 10 minutes.

3. Combine 1½ cups flour, baking powder, cinnamon and salt in large bowl; stir in raisins. Whisk sugar, eggs, ½ cup butter and vanilla in separate medium bowl; stir in oat mixture. Pour sugar mixture into flour mixture; stir just until moistened. Pour into prepared pan. Place in **CROCK-POT®** slow cooker. Cover; cook on HIGH 2½ to 3 hours or until toothpick inserted into center comes out clean.

4. Remove bread from **CROCK-POT®** slow cooker; let cool in pan 10 minutes. Remove bread from pan; let cool on wire rack 3 minutes before slicing. Serve with additional butter, if desired.

Mediterranean Frittata

Makes 4 to 6 servings

Butter, softened

3 tablespoons extra virgin olive oil

1 large onion, chopped

8 ounces (about 2 cups) sliced mushrooms

6 cloves garlic, sliced

1 teaspoon dried basil

1 medium red bell pepper, chopped

1 package (10 ounces) frozen chopped spinach, thawed and squeezed dry

¼ cup sliced kalamata olives

8 eggs, beaten

4 ounces feta cheese, crumbled

½ teaspoon salt

¼ teaspoon black pepper

1. Coat inside of 5- to 6-quart **CROCK-POT**® slow cooker with butter. Heat oil in large skillet over medium-high heat. Add onion, mushrooms, garlic and basil; cook 2 to 3 minutes or until slightly softened, stirring occasionally. Add bell pepper; cook 4 to 5 minutes or until vegetables are tender. Stir in spinach; cook 2 minutes. Stir in olives. Remove onion mixture to **CROCK-POT**® slow cooker.

2. Whisk eggs, cheese, salt and black pepper in large bowl. Pour over vegetables in **CROCK-POT**® slow cooker. Cover; cook on LOW 2½ to 3 hours or on HIGH 1¼ to 1½ hours or until eggs are set. Cut into wedges to serve.

Farro Risotto with Mushrooms and Spinach

Makes 4 servings

2 tablespoons olive oil, divided

1 onion, chopped

12 ounces cremini mushrooms, stems trimmed and quartered

¾ teaspoon salt

¼ teaspoon black pepper

2 cloves garlic, minced

1 cup farro

1 sprig fresh thyme

4 cups vegetable broth

8 ounces baby spinach

½ cup grated Parmesan cheese

1. Heat 1 tablespoon oil in large skillet over medium heat. Add onion; cook 8 minutes or until tender. Remove to **CROCK-POT®** slow cooker. Add remaining 1 tablespoon oil to same skillet; heat over medium-high heat. Add mushrooms, salt and pepper; cook 6 to 8 minutes or until mushrooms have released their liquid and are browned. Add garlic; cook 1 minute. Stir in farro and thyme; cook 1 minute. Remove mushroom mixture to **CROCK-POT®** slow cooker.

2. Stir broth into **CROCK-POT®** slow cooker. Cover; cook on HIGH 3½ hours until farro is tender and broth is absorbed. Remove thyme sprig. Stir in spinach and cheese just before serving.

Black Bean, Zucchini and Corn Enchiladas

Makes 6 servings

1 tablespoon vegetable oil

1 medium onion, chopped

2 medium zucchini

2 cups corn

1 large red bell pepper, chopped

1 teaspoon minced garlic

½ teaspoon salt

½ teaspoon ground cumin

¼ teaspoon ground coriander

1 can (about 14 ounces) black beans, rinsed and drained

2 jars (16 ounces *each*) salsa verde

12 (6-inch) corn tortillas

2½ cups (10 ounces) shredded Monterey Jack cheese

2 tablespoons chopped fresh cilantro

1. Heat oil in large skillet over medium heat. Add onion; cook 6 minutes or until softened. Add zucchini, corn and bell pepper; cook 2 minutes. Add garlic, salt, cumin and coriander; cook and stir 1 minute. Stir in beans. Remove from heat.

2. Pour 1 cup salsa in bottom of **CROCK-POT**® slow cooker. Arrange 3 tortillas in single layer, cutting the tortillas in half as needed to make them fit. Place 2 cups vegetable mixture over tortillas; sprinkle with ½ cup cheese. Repeat layering two more times. Layer with remaining 3 tortillas; top with 2 cups salsa. Sprinkle with remaining 1 cup cheese. Reserve remaining filling for another use.

3. Cover; cook on HIGH 2 hours or until cheese is bubbly and edges are lightly browned. Sprinkle with cilantro. Turn off heat. Let stand, uncovered, 10 minutes before serving.

Chickpea and Vegetable Curry

Makes 4 servings

1 can (14 ounces) unsweetened coconut milk

1 cup vegetable broth, divided

2 teaspoons curry powder

¼ teaspoon ground red pepper

2 cups cut fresh green beans (1-inch pieces)

1 can (about 15 ounces) chickpeas, rinsed and drained

2 carrots, thinly sliced

½ cup golden raisins

¼ cup all-purpose flour

2 cups hot cooked couscous

Green onion and toasted sliced almonds (optional)

1. Coat inside of **CROCK-POT®** slow cooker with nonstick cooking spray. Combine coconut milk, ¾ cup broth, curry powder and ground red pepper in **CROCK-POT®** slow cooker. Stir in green beans, chickpeas, carrots and raisins. Cover; cook on LOW 6 to 7 hours or on HIGH 2½ to 3 hours.

2. Stir remaining ¼ cup broth into flour in small bowl until smooth. Stir into vegetable mixture. Cover; cook on HIGH 15 minutes or until thickened. Ladle into shallow bowls; top with couscous, green onion and almonds, if desired.

Tofu Tikka Masala

Makes 4 to 6 servings

1 package (14 to 16 ounces) extra firm tofu, cut into 1-inch pieces

½ cup whole milk yogurt

2 teaspoons salt, divided

1 tablespoon plus 1 teaspoon minced garlic, divided

2½ teaspoons grated fresh ginger, divided

2 tablespoons vegetable oil

1 medium onion, chopped

2 tablespoons tomato paste

1 tablespoon garam masala

1 can (28 ounces) crushed tomatoes

1 teaspoon sugar

½ cup whipping cream

3 tablespoons chopped fresh cilantro

Hot cooked basmati rice

1. Combine tofu, yogurt, 1 teaspoon salt, 1 teaspoon garlic and 1 teaspoon ginger in large bowl; stir to blend. Cover; refrigerate 1 hour or overnight.

2. Heat oil in large skillet over medium heat. Add onion; cook 8 minutes or until softened. Add remaining 1 tablespoon garlic, remaining 1½ teaspoons ginger, tomato paste, remaining 1 teaspoon salt and garam masala; cook and stir 1 minute. Add tomatoes and sugar; bring to a simmer. Remove onion mixture and tofu to **CROCK-POT®** slow cooker using slotted spoon; stir to combine.

3. Cover; cook on LOW 8 hours. Stir in cream and cilantro. Serve over rice.

Eggplant Parmesan

Makes 4 servings

¼ **cup all-purpose flour**

1 **teaspoon dried oregano**

1 **teaspoon dried basil**

½ **teaspoon salt**

1 **egg**

2 **teaspoons cold water**

2 **tablespoons extra virgin olive oil, divided**

1 **large eggplant (about 1 pound), ends trimmed, peeled and cut crosswise into 8 slices**

2¼ **cups spicy marinara pasta sauce**

½ **cup panko bread crumbs**

1½ **cups (6 ounces) shredded Italian cheese blend or mozzarella cheese**

Chopped fresh basil (optional)

1. Combine flour, oregano, dried basil and salt in shallow dish or pie plate. Beat egg with water in another shallow dish or pie plate.

2. Heat 1 tablespoon oil in large skillet over medium heat. Dip each slice of eggplant in egg mixture, letting excess drip back into dish. Dredge in flour mixture, coating both sides lightly. Cook 4 slices 3 to 4 minutes per side or until lightly browned. Repeat with remaining oil and 4 slices eggplant.

3. Coat inside of **CROCK-POT®** slow cooker with nonstick cooking spray. Layer ¾ cup pasta sauce in bottom of **CROCK-POT®** slow cooker. Arrange 4 slices of browned eggplant over sauce, overlapping if necessary. Top with ¼ cup bread crumbs and ½ cup cheese. Repeat layering with ¾ cup pasta sauce, 4 slices eggplant, ¼ cup bread crumbs and ½ cup cheese. Spoon remaining pasta sauce over cheese. Cover; cook on LOW 4 to 5 hours or on HIGH 2 to 2½ hours.

4. Sprinkle remaining ½ cup cheese on top. Turn off heat. Let stand, covered, 5 minutes or until cheese is melted. Garnish with fresh basil.

Vegetable-Bean Pasta Sauce

Makes 8 servings

2 cans (about 15 ounces *each*) cannellini beans, rinsed and drained

2 cans (about 14 ounces *each*) diced tomatoes

16 baby carrots

1 medium onion, sliced

1 can (6 ounces) tomato paste

1 ounce dried oyster mushrooms, chopped

¼ cup grated Parmesan cheese

2 teaspoons garlic powder

1 teaspoon dried basil

1 teaspoon dried oregano

½ teaspoon dried rosemary

½ teaspoon dried marjoram

½ teaspoon dried sage

½ teaspoon dried thyme

¼ teaspoon black pepper

1 package (12 ounces) whole wheat spaghetti, cooked and drained

1. Combine beans, tomatoes, carrots, onion, tomato paste, mushrooms, cheese, garlic powder, basil, oregano, rosemary, marjoram, sage, thyme and pepper in **CROCK-POT**® slow cooker; stir to blend.

2. Cover; cook on LOW 8 to 10 hours. Serve over spaghetti.

Italian Eggplant with Millet and Pepper Stuffing

Makes 4 servings

¼ cup uncooked millet

2 small eggplants (about ¾ pound total), unpeeled

¼ cup chopped red bell pepper, divided

¼ cup chopped green bell pepper, divided

1 teaspoon olive oil

1 clove garlic, minced

1½ cups vegetable broth

½ teaspoon ground cumin

½ teaspoon dried oregano

⅛ teaspoon red pepper flakes

Sprigs fresh basil (optional)

1. Heat large skillet over medium heat. Add millet; cook and stir 5 minutes. Remove to small bowl; set aside. Cut eggplants lengthwise into halves. Scoop out flesh, leaving about ¼-inch-thick shell. Reserve shells; chop eggplant flesh. Combine 1 tablespoon red bell pepper and 1 tablespoon green bell pepper in small bowl; set aside.

2. Heat oil in same skillet over medium heat. Add chopped eggplant, remaining red and green bell peppers and garlic; cook and stir 8 minutes or until eggplant is tender.

3. Combine eggplant mixture, broth, cumin, oregano and red pepper flakes in **CROCK-POT**® slow cooker. Cover; cook on LOW 4½ hours or until all liquid is absorbed.

4. Turn **CROCK-POT**® slow cooker to HIGH. Fill eggplant shells with eggplant-millet mixture. Sprinkle with reserved bell peppers. Place filled shells in **CROCK-POT**® slow cooker. Cover; cook on HIGH 1½ to 2 hours. Garnish with basil.

Thai Red Curry with Tofu

Makes 4 servings

1 medium sweet potato, peeled and cut into 1-inch pieces

1 small eggplant, halved lengthwise and cut crosswise into ½-inch-wide halves

8 ounces extra firm tofu, cut into 1-inch pieces

½ cup green beans, cut into 1-inch pieces

½ red bell pepper, cut into ¼-inch-wide strips

2 tablespoons vegetable oil

5 medium shallots (about 1½ cups), thinly sliced

3 tablespoons Thai red curry paste

1 teaspoon minced garlic

1 teaspoon grated ginger

1 can (about 13 ounces) coconut milk

1½ tablespoons soy sauce

1 tablespoon light brown sugar

¼ cup chopped fresh basil leaves

2 tablespoons lime juice

Hot cooked rice (optional)

1. Coat inside of **CROCK-POT®** slow cooker with nonstick cooking spray. Add sweet potato, eggplant, tofu, green beans and bell pepper.

2. Heat oil in large skillet over medium heat. Add shallots; cook 5 minutes or until browned and tender. Add curry paste, garlic and ginger; cook and stir 1 minute. Add coconut milk, soy sauce and brown sugar; bring to a simmer. Pour mixture over vegetables in **CROCK-POT®** slow cooker.

3. Cover; cook on LOW 2 to 3 hours. Stir in basil and lime juice. Serve over rice, if desired.

Summer Squash Lasagna

Makes 6 to 8 servings

3 tablespoons olive oil, divided

1 large onion, chopped

¾ teaspoon salt, divided

2 cloves garlic, minced

2 medium zucchini (about 1 pound), cut lengthwise into ¼-inch strips

2 yellow squash (about 1 pound), cut lengthwise into ¼-inch strips

1 container (15 ounces) ricotta cheese

1 egg

¼ cup plus 2 tablespoons chopped fresh basil, divided

¼ teaspoon black pepper

½ cup grated Parmesan cheese, divided

1 jar (24 to 26 ounces) marinara sauce

1 package (8 ounces) shredded mozzarella cheese, divided

12 uncooked lasagna noodles

1. Coat inside of **CROCK-POT®** slow cooker with nonstick cooking spray. Heat 1 tablespoon oil in large skillet over medium-high heat. Add onion and ¼ teaspoon salt; cook and stir 5 minutes or until tender. Add garlic; cook and stir 1 minute. Remove to large bowl.

2. Heat 1 tablespoon oil in same skillet. Add zucchini and ¼ teaspoon salt; cook and stir 5 minutes or until lightly browned. Remove mixture to bowl with onion. Repeat with remaining 1 tablespoon oil, squash and remaining ¼ teaspoon salt. Combine ricotta cheese, egg, ¼ cup basil, pepper and ¼ cup Parmesan cheese in medium bowl; stir to blend.

3. Pour ½ cup marinara sauce evenly into bottom of **CROCK-POT®** slow cooker. Layer 3 lasagna noodles (break to fit evenly); top with ⅔ cup ricotta mixture, ⅓ squash mixture, ¼ cup mozzarella and ½ cup marinara sauce. Repeat layers 2 times. Top with remaining 3 lasagna noodles, marinara sauce and mozzarella. Sprinkle with remaining ¼ cup Parmesan cheese.

4. Cover; cook on LOW 3 hours. Turn off heat. Uncover; let stand 30 minutes. Sprinkle with remaining 2 tablespoons basil before cutting.

Corn Bread and Bean Casserole

Makes 8 servings

Filling

- **1 medium onion, chopped**
- **1 medium green bell pepper, diced**
- **2 cloves garlic, minced**
- **1 can (about 15 ounces) red kidney beans, rinsed and drained**
- **1 can (about 15 ounces) pinto beans, rinsed and drained**
- **1 can (about 15 ounces) diced tomatoes with mild green chiles**
- **1 can (8 ounces) tomato sauce**
- **1 teaspoon chili powder**
- **½ teaspoon ground cumin**
- **½ teaspoon black pepper**
- **¼ teaspoon hot pepper sauce**

Topping

- **1 cup yellow cornmeal**
- **1 cup all-purpose flour**
- **2½ teaspoons baking powder**
- **1 tablespoon sugar**
- **½ teaspoon salt**
- **1 can (8½ ounces) cream-style corn**
- **1¼ cups milk**
- **2 eggs**
- **3 tablespoons vegetable oil**

1. Coat inside of **CROCK-POT®** slow cooker with nonstick cooking spray. Heat large skillet over medium heat. Add onion, bell pepper and garlic; cook and stir 5 minutes or until tender. Remove to **CROCK-POT®** slow cooker.

2. Stir beans, diced tomatoes, tomato sauce, chili powder, cumin, black pepper and hot pepper sauce into **CROCK-POT®** slow cooker. Cover; cook on HIGH 1 hour.

3. Combine cornmeal, flour, baking powder, sugar and salt in large bowl. Stir in corn, milk, eggs and oil; mix well. Spoon evenly over bean mixture in **CROCK-POT®** slow cooker. Cover; cook on HIGH 1½ to 2 hours or until corn bread topping is golden brown.

Ziti Ratatouille

Makes 6 to 8 servings

1 large eggplant, cut into ½-inch cubes (about 1½ pounds)

2 zucchini, cut into ½-inch cubes

1 green or red bell pepper, cut into ½-inch pieces

1 onion, chopped

4 cloves garlic, minced

1 jar (24 to 26 ounces) pasta sauce

2 cans (about 14 ounces *each*) diced tomatoes with garlic and onions

1 package (8 ounces) uncooked ziti pasta

1 can (6 ounces) pitted black olives, drained

Lemon juice

Shaved Parmesan cheese (optional)

1. Place eggplant, zucchini, bell pepper, onion, garlic, pasta sauce and tomatoes in **CROCK-POT®** slow cooker. Cover; cook on LOW 4½ hours.

2. Stir in pasta and olives. Cover; cook on LOW 25 minutes or until pasta is tender. Drizzle with lemon juice and sprinkle with cheese, if desired.

No-Fuss Macaroni and Cheese

Makes 6 to 8 servings

2 cups (about 8 ounces) uncooked
   elbow macaroni

4 ounces pasteurized process
   cheese product, cubed

1 cup (4 ounces) shredded mild
   Cheddar cheese

½ teaspoon salt

⅛ teaspoon black pepper

1½ cups milk

Combine macaroni, cheese product, Cheddar cheese, salt and pepper in **CROCK-POT®** slow cooker. Pour in milk. Cover; cook on LOW 2 to 3 hours, stirring after 20 to 30 minutes.

Chicken and Vegetable Soup

Makes 10 servings

1 tablespoon olive oil

2 medium parsnips, cut into ½-inch pieces

2 medium carrots, cut into ½-inch pieces

2 medium onions, chopped

2 stalks celery, cut into ½-inch pieces

1 cut-up whole chicken (3 to 3½ pounds)

4 cups chicken broth

10 sprigs fresh Italian parsley *or* 1½ teaspoons dried parsley flakes

4 sprigs fresh thyme *or* ½ teaspoon dried thyme

1. Coat inside of **CROCK-POT®** slow cooker with nonstick cooking spray. Heat oil in large skillet over medium-high heat. Add parsnips, carrots, onions and celery; cook and stir 5 minutes or until vegetables are softened. Remove parsnip mixture to **CROCK-POT®** slow cooker. Add chicken, broth, parsley and thyme.

2. Cover; cook on LOW 6 to 7 hours. Remove chicken to large cutting board; let stand 10 minutes. Remove and discard skin and bones from chicken. Shred chicken using two forks. Stir shredded chicken into **CROCK-POT®** slow cooker.

Three-Bean Chili with Chorizo

Makes 6 to 8 servings

2 Mexican chorizo sausages (about 6 ounces *each*), removed from casings

1 tablespoon vegetable oil

1 large onion, chopped

1 tablespoon salt

1 tablespoon minced garlic

1 tablespoon tomato paste

2 to 3 teaspoons chili powder

2 to 3 teaspoons ancho chili powder

2 to 3 teaspoons chipotle chili powder

2 teaspoons ground cumin

1 teaspoon ground coriander

3 cups water

2 cans (about 14 ounces *each*) crushed tomatoes

½ cup dried pinto beans, rinsed and sorted

½ cup dried kidney beans, rinsed and sorted

½ cup dried black beans, rinsed and sorted

Chopped fresh cilantro (optional)

1. Heat large nonstick skillet over medium-high heat. Add sausage; cook 3 to 4 minutes, stirring to break up meat. Remove to **CROCK-POT®** slow cooker using slotted spoon.

2. Wipe out skillet. Heat oil over medium heat. Add onion; cook 6 minutes or until softened. Add salt, garlic, tomato paste, chili powders, cumin and coriander; cook and stir 1 minute. Remove onion mixture to **CROCK-POT®** slow cooker. Stir in water, tomatoes and beans.

3. Cover; cook on LOW 10 hours. Garnish each serving with cilantro.

Beef and Beet Borscht

Makes 6 to 8 servings

6 slices bacon

1 boneless beef chuck roast (1½ pounds), trimmed and cut into ½-inch pieces

1 medium onion, chopped

4 cloves garlic, minced

4 medium beets, peeled and cut into ½-inch pieces

2 large carrots, sliced

3 cups beef broth

6 sprigs fresh dill

3 tablespoons honey

3 tablespoons red wine vinegar

2 whole bay leaves

3 cups shredded green cabbage

1. Heat large skillet over medium heat. Add bacon; cook until crisp-cooked and tender. Remove to papertowel lined plate; crumble.

2. Return skillet to medium-high heat. Add beef; cook 5 minutes or until browned. Remove beef to **CROCK-POT**® slow cooker.

3. Pour off all but 1 tablespoon fat from skillet. Add onion and garlic; cook 4 minutes or until onion is softened. Remove onion mixture to **CROCK-POT**® slow cooker. Stir in beets, carrots, broth, bacon, dill, honey, vinegar and bay leaves. Cover; cook on LOW 5 to 6 hours. Stir in cabbage. Cover; cook on LOW 30 minutes.

Turkey Chili

Makes 6 servings

2 tablespoons olive oil, divided

1½ pounds ground turkey

2 medium onions, chopped

1 medium red bell pepper, chopped

1 medium green bell pepper, chopped

5 cloves garlic, minced

1 jalapeño pepper, finely chopped*

2 cans (about 14 ounces *each*) fire-roasted diced tomatoes

4 teaspoons chili powder

1 teaspoon ground cumin

1 teaspoon dried oregano

½ teaspoon salt

*Jalapeño peppers can sting and irritate the skin, so wear rubber gloves when handling peppers and do not touch your eyes.

1. Heat 1 tablespoon oil in large skillet over medium-high heat. Add turkey; cook 7 to 8 minutes, stirring to break up meat. Remove to **CROCK-POT®** slow cooker using slotted spoon.

2. Heat remaining 1 tablespoon oil in same skillet over medium-high heat. Add onions, bell peppers, garlic and jalapeño pepper; cook and stir 4 to 5 minutes or until softened. Stir in tomatoes, chili powder, cumin, oregano and salt; cook 1 minute. Remove onion mixture to **CROCK-POT®** slow cooker. Cover; cook on LOW 6 hours.

Easy Beef Stew

Makes 6 to 8 servings

1½ to 2 pounds cubed beef stew meat

4 medium potatoes, cubed

4 carrots, cut into 1½-inch pieces *or* 4 cups baby carrots

1 medium onion, cut into 8 pieces

2 cans (8 ounces *each*) tomato sauce

1 teaspoon salt

½ teaspoon black pepper

Chopped fresh cilantro (optional)

Combine beef, potatoes, carrots, onion, tomato sauce, salt and pepper in **CROCK-POT®** slow cooker. Cover; cook on LOW 8 to 10 hours. Garnish with cilantro.

Shrimp and Okra Gumbo

Makes 6 servings

1 tablespoon olive oil

8 ounces kielbasa, halved lengthwise and cut into ¼-inch-thick half moons

1 green bell pepper, chopped

1 medium onion, chopped

3 stalks celery, cut into ¼-inch slices

6 green onions, chopped

4 cloves garlic, minced

1 cup chicken broth

1 can (about 14 ounces) diced tomatoes

1 teaspoon Cajun seasoning

½ teaspoon dried thyme

1 pound large shrimp, peeled and deveined (with tails on)

2 cups frozen cut okra, thawed

1. Coat inside of **CROCK-POT®** slow cooker with nonstick cooking spray. Heat oil in large skillet over medium-high heat. Add kielbasa; cook and stir 4 minutes or until browned. Remove to **CROCK-POT®** slow cooker using slotted spoon.

2. Return skillet to medium-high heat. Add bell pepper, chopped onion, celery, green onions and garlic; cook and stir 5 to 6 minutes or until vegetables are crisp-tender. Remove to **CROCK-POT®** slow cooker. Stir in broth, tomatoes, Cajun seasoning and thyme.

3. Cover; cook on LOW 4 hours. Stir in shrimp and okra. Cover; cook on LOW 30 minutes.

Chicken and Mushroom Stew

Makes 6 servings

4 tablespoons vegetable oil, divided

2 medium leeks, white and light green parts only, halved lengthwise and sliced crosswise

1 carrot, cut into 1-inch pieces

1 stalk celery, diced

6 chicken thighs (about 2 pounds)

Salt and black pepper

12 ounces cremini mushrooms, quartered

1 ounce dried porcini mushrooms, rehydrated in 1½ cups hot water and chopped, soaking liquid strained and reserved

1 teaspoon minced garlic

1 sprig fresh thyme

1 whole bay leaf

¼ cup all-purpose flour

½ cup dry white wine

1 cup chicken broth

1. Heat 1 tablespoon oil in large skillet over medium heat. Add leeks; cook 8 minutes or until softened. Remove to **CROCK-POT®** slow cooker. Add carrot and celery.

2. Heat 1 tablespoon oil in same skillet over medium-high heat. Season chicken with salt and pepper. Add chicken in batches; cook 8 minutes or until browned on both sides. Remove to **CROCK-POT®** slow cooker.

3. Heat remaining 2 tablespoons oil in same skillet. Add cremini mushrooms; cook 7 minutes or until mushrooms have released their liquid and started to brown. Add porcini mushrooms, garlic, thyme, bay leaf and flour; cook and stir 1 minute. Add wine; cook and stir until evaporated, stirring to scrape any browned bits from bottom of skillet. Add reserved soaking liquid and broth; bring to a simmer. Pour mixture into **CROCK-POT®** slow cooker.

4. Cover; cook on HIGH 2 to 3 hours. Remove and discard thyme sprig and bay leaf.

Pozole Rojo

Makes 8 servings

4 dried ancho chiles, stemmed
and seeded

3 dried guajillo chiles, stemmed
and seeded*

2 cups boiling water

2½ pounds boneless pork shoulder
roast, cut in half

3 teaspoons salt, divided

1 tablespoon vegetable oil

2 medium onions, chopped

1½ tablespoons minced garlic

2 teaspoons ground cumin

2 teaspoons Mexican oregano**

4 cups chicken broth

2 cans (30 ounces *each*) white
hominy, rinsed and drained

Sliced radishes (optional)

*Guajillo chiles can be found in the ethnic
section of most large supermarkets.*

**Mexican oregano has a much stronger
flavor than regular oregano.*

1. Place ancho and guajillo chiles in medium bowl; pour boiling water over top. Weigh down chiles with small plate; soak 30 minutes. Season pork with 1 teaspoon salt. Heat oil in large skillet over medium-high heat. Add pork; cook 8 to 10 minutes or until browned on all sides. Remove to pork to **CROCK-POT**® slow cooker.

2. Heat same skillet over medium heat. Add onions; cook 6 minutes or until softened. Add garlic, cumin, oregano and remaining 2 teaspoons salt; cook and stir 1 minute. Stir in broth; bring to a simmer, scraping up any browned bits from bottom of skillet. Remove to **CROCK-POT**® slow cooker.

3. Place softened chiles and soaking liquid in food processor or blender; blend until smooth. Pour through fine-mesh sieve into medium bowl. Discard solids. Stir mixture into **CROCK-POT**® slow cooker.

4. Cover; cook on LOW 5 hours. Stir in hominy. Cover; cook on LOW 1 hour. Turn off heat. Let stand 10 to 15 minutes. Skim off fat and discard. Remove pork to large cutting board; shred with two forks. Top each serving with pork and radishes, if desired.

Lamb and Chickpea Stew

Makes 6 servings

2 tablespoons vegetable oil, divided

1 pound lamb stew meat

2 teaspoons salt, divided

1 large onion, chopped

1 tablespoon minced garlic

1½ teaspoons ground cumin

1 teaspoon ground coriander

1 teaspoon ground turmeric

1 teaspoon ground cinnamon

¼ teaspoon black pepper

2 cups chicken broth

1 cup diced canned tomatoes, drained

1 cup dry chickpeas, rinsed and sorted

½ cup chopped dried apricots

¼ cup chopped fresh Italian parsley

2 tablespoons honey

2 tablespoons lemon juice

Hot cooked couscous

1. Heat 1 tablespoon oil in large skillet over medium-high heat. Season lamb with 1 teaspoon salt. Add lamb; cook 8 minutes or until browned on all sides. Remove lamb mixture to **CROCK-POT®** slow cooker.

2. Heat remaining 1 tablespoon oil in same skillet over medium heat. Add onion; cook 6 minutes or until softened. Add garlic, remaining 1 teaspoon salt, cumin, coriander, turmeric, cinnamon and pepper; cook and stir 1 minute. Add broth and tomatoes; cook and stir 5 minutes, scraping up any brown bits from bottom of skillet. Remove onion mixture to **CROCK-POT®** slow cooker. Stir in chickpeas.

3. Cover; cook on LOW 7 hours. Stir in apricots. Cover; cook on LOW 1 hour. Turn off heat. Let stand 10 minutes. Skim off and discard fat. Stir in parsley, honey and lemon juice. Serve with couscous.

Broccoli Cheddar Soup

Makes 6 servings

3 tablespoons unsalted butter

1 medium onion, chopped

3 tablespoons all-purpose flour

¼ teaspoon ground nutmeg

¼ teaspoon black pepper

4 cups vegetable broth

1 large bunch broccoli, chopped

1 medium red potato, peeled and chopped

1 teaspoon salt

1 whole bay leaf

1½ cups (6 ounces) shredded Cheddar cheese, plus additional for garnish

½ cup whipping cream

1. Melt butter in medium saucepan over medium heat. Add onion; cook 6 minutes or until onion is softened. Add flour, nutmeg and pepper; cook and stir 1 minute. Remove to **CROCK-POT**® slow cooker. Stir in broth, broccoli, potato, salt and bay leaf.

2. Cover; cook on HIGH 3 hours. Remove and discard bay leaf. Add soup in batches to food processor or blender; purée until desired consistency. (Or, use an immersion blender.) Pour soup back into **CROCK-POT**® slow cooker. Stir in 1½ cups cheese and cream until cheese is melted. Garnish with additional cheese.

Texas Chili

Makes 8 servings

4 tablespoons vegetable oil, divided

3½ to 4 pounds cubed beef stew meat

Salt and black pepper

1 large onion, diced

¼ cup chili powder

1 tablespoon ground cumin

1 tablespoon tomato paste

1 tablespoon minced garlic

2 teaspoons ground coriander

1 teaspoon dried oregano

3 cans (about 14 ounces *each*) diced tomatoes

3 tablespoons cornmeal or masa harina

1 tablespoon packed light brown sugar

1. Heat 3 tablespoons oil in large skillet over medium-high heat. Season beef with salt and pepper. Add beef in batches; cook 8 minutes or until browned. Remove to **CROCK-POT**® slow cooker.

2. Heat remaining 1 tablespoon oil in same skillet. Add onion; cook and stir 6 minutes or until softened. Stir in chili powder, cumin, tomato paste, garlic, coriander and oregano. Season with salt and pepper; cook and stir 1 minute. Stir in tomatoes, cornmeal and brown sugar; bring to a simmer. Remove to **CROCK-POT**® slow cooker. Cover; cook on LOW 7 to 8 hours.

Variation: Add ¼ teaspoon ground red pepper, if a spicier chili is desired.

White Chicken Chili

Makes 6 to 8 servings

8 ounces dried navy beans, rinsed and sorted

1 tablespoon vegetable oil

2 pounds boneless, skinless chicken breasts (about 4)

2 onions, chopped

1 tablespoon minced garlic

2 teaspoons ground cumin

2 teaspoons salt

1 teaspoon dried oregano

¼ teaspoon black pepper

¼ teaspoon ground red pepper (optional)

4 cups chicken broth

1 can (4 ounces) fire-roasted diced mild green chiles, rinsed and drained

¼ cup chopped fresh cilantro

Tortilla chips (optional)

Lime wedges (optional)

1. Place beans on bottom of **CROCK-POT®** slow cooker. Heat oil in large skillet over medium-high heat. Add chicken; cook 8 minutes or until browned on all sides. Remove to **CROCK-POT®** slow cooker.

2. Heat same skillet over medium heat. Add onions; cook 6 minutes or until softened and lightly browned. Add garlic, cumin, salt, oregano, black pepper and ground red pepper, if desired; cook and stir 1 minute. Add broth and chiles; bring to a simmer, stirring to scrape up any browned bits from bottom of skillet. Remove onion mixture to **CROCK-POT®** slow cooker.

3. Cover; cook on LOW 5 hours. Remove chicken to large cutting board; shred with two forks. Return chicken to **CROCK-POT®** slow cooker. Stir in cilantro. Serve with chips and lime, if desired.

Braised Short Ribs with Aromatic Spices

Makes 4 servings

1 tablespoon olive oil

3 pounds bone-in beef short ribs, trimmed

1 teaspoon ground cumin, divided

1 teaspoon salt, divided

½ teaspoon black pepper, divided

2 medium onions, halved and thinly sliced

10 cloves garlic, thinly sliced

2 tablespoons balsamic vinegar

2 tablespoons honey

1 whole cinnamon stick

2 star anise pods

2 large sweet potatoes, peeled and cut into ¾-inch cubes

1 cup beef broth

1. Heat oil in large skillet over medium-high heat. Season ribs with ½ teaspoon cumin, ¾ teaspoon salt and ¼ teaspoon pepper. Add to skillet; cook 8 minutes or until browned, turning occasionally. Remove ribs to large plate.

2. Heat same skillet over medium heat. Add onions and garlic; cook 12 to 14 minutes or until onions are lightly browned. Stir in vinegar; cook 1 minute. Add remaining ½ teaspoon cumin, honey, cinnamon stick and star anise; cook and stir 30 seconds. Remove mixture to **CROCK-POT®** slow cooker. Stir in potatoes; top with ribs. Pour in broth.

3. Cover; cook on LOW 8 to 9 hours or until meat is falling off the bones. Remove and discard bones from ribs. Remove and discard cinnamon stick and star anise. Turn off heat. Let mixture stand 5 to 10 minutes. Skim off and discard fat. Serve meat with sauce and vegetables.

Easy Salisbury Steak

Makes 4 servings

1½ pounds ground beef

1 egg

½ cup plain dry bread crumbs

1 package (1 ounce) onion soup mix*

1 can (10½ ounces) golden mushroom soup, undiluted

Hot cooked mashed potatoes and asparagus

You may pulse onion soup mix in a small food processor or coffee grinder for a finer grind, if desired.

1. Coat inside of **CROCK-POT®** slow cooker with nonstick cooking spray. Combine beef, egg, bread crumbs and dry onion soup mix in large bowl. Form mixture evenly into four 1-inch thick patties.

2. Heat large skillet over medium-high heat. Add patties; cook 2 minutes per side or until lightly browned. Remove to **CROCK-POT®** slow cooker, in single layer. Spread mushroom soup evenly over patties. Cover; cook on LOW 3 to 3½ hours. Serve with potatoes and asparagus, if desired.

Shrimp Jambalaya

Makes 8 servings

1 (8-ounce) box New Orleans style jambalaya mix

2½ cups water

1 can (about 14 ounces) diced tomatoes with green pepper, celery and onion

8 ounces andouille sausage, cut into ¼-inch-thick slices

1 teaspoon hot pepper sauce, plus additional for serving

1½ pounds large shrimp, peeled and deveined (with tails on)

1. Coat inside of **CROCK-POT®** slow cooker with nonstick cooking spray. Add jambalaya mix, water, tomatoes, sausage and 1 teaspoon hot pepper sauce; stir to blend. Cover; cook on LOW 2½ to 3 hours or until rice absorbs most of the liquid.

2. Stir in shrimp. Cover; cook on LOW 30 minutes or until shrimp are cooked through. Serve with additional hot pepper sauce.

Maple-Dry Rubbed Ribs

Makes 4 servings

2 teaspoons chili powder, divided

1 teaspoon ground coriander

1 teaspoon garlic powder, divided

½ teaspoon salt

¼ teaspoon black pepper

3 to 3½ pounds pork baby back ribs, trimmed and cut in half

3 tablespoons maple syrup, divided

1 can (about 8 ounces) tomato sauce

¼ teaspoon ground cinnamon

¼ teaspoon ground ginger

1. Coat inside of **CROCK-POT®** slow cooker with nonstick cooking spray. Combine 1 teaspoon chili powder, coriander, ½ teaspoon garlic powder, salt and pepper in small bowl; stir to blend. Brush ribs with 1 tablespoon syrup; rub with spice mixture. Remove ribs in **CROCK-POT®** slow cooker.

2. Combine tomato sauce, remaining 1 teaspoon chili powder, ½ teaspoon garlic powder, 2 tablespoons maple syrup, cinnamon and ginger in medium bowl; stir to blend. Pour tomato sauce mixture over ribs in **CROCK-POT®** slow cooker. Cover; cook on LOW 8 to 9 hours.

3. Remove ribs to large serving platter; cover with foil to keep warm. Turn **CROCK-POT®** slow cooker to HIGH. Cook, uncovered, 10 to 15 minutes or until sauce is thickened. Brush ribs with sauce and serve any remaining sauce on the side.

Pineapple and Butternut Squash Braised Chicken

Makes 4 servings

1 medium butternut squash, cut into 1-inch pieces (about 3 cups)

1 can (20 ounces) pineapple chunks, undrained

½ cup ketchup

2 tablespoons packed brown sugar

8 chicken thighs (about 2 pounds)

½ teaspoon salt

¼ teaspoon black pepper

1. Coat inside of **CROCK-POT®** slow cooker with nonstick cooking spray. Combine squash, pineapple with juice, ketchup and brown sugar in **CROCK-POT®** slow cooker. Season chicken with salt and pepper. Place chicken on top of squash mixture.

2. Cover; cook on LOW 5 to 6 hours. Remove chicken to large platter; cover loosely with foil. Turn **CROCK-POT®** slow cooker to HIGH. Cook, uncovered, on HIGH 10 to 15 minutes or until thickened. Serve sauce over chicken.

Pulled Pork with Honey-Chipotle Barbecue Sauce

Makes 8 servings

3 teaspoons chili powder, divided

1 teaspoon chipotle chili powder, divided

1 teaspoon ground cumin, divided

1 teaspoon garlic powder, divided

1 teaspoon salt

1 (3½-pound) bone-in pork shoulder, trimmed

1 can (15 ounces) tomato sauce

5 tablespoons honey, divided

1. Coat inside of **CROCK-POT®** slow cooker with nonstick cooking spray. Combine 1 teaspoon chili powder, ½ teaspoon chipotle chili powder, ½ teaspoon cumin, ½ teaspoon garlic powder and salt in small bowl. Rub pork with chili powder mixture. Place pork in **CROCK-POT®** slow cooker.

2. Combine tomato sauce, 4 tablespoons honey, remaining 2 teaspoons chili powder, ½ teaspoon chipotle chili powder, ½ teaspoon cumin and ½ teaspoon garlic powder in large bowl; stir to blend. Pour tomato mixture over pork in **CROCK-POT®** slow cooker. Cover; cook on LOW 8 hours.

3. Remove pork to large bowl; cover loosely with foil. Turn **CROCK-POT®** slow cooker to HIGH. Cover; cook on HIGH 30 minutes or until sauce is thickened. Stir in remaining 1 tablespoon honey.

4. Remove bone from pork and discard. Shred pork using two forks. Stir shredded pork into **CROCK-POT®** slow cooker to coat with sauce.

Beef and Quinoa Stuffed Cabbage Rolls

Makes 4 servings

8 large green cabbage leaves, veins trimmed at bottom of each leaf

1 pound ground beef

1½ cups cooked quinoa

1 medium onion, chopped

1 cup tomato juice, divided

Salt and black pepper

1. Heat salted water in large saucepan over high heat; bring to a boil. Add cabbage leaves; return to boil. Cook 2 minutes. Drain and let cool.

2. Combine beef, quinoa, onion, ¼ cup tomato juice, salt and pepper in large bowl; mix well. Place cabbage leaf on large work surface; top center with 2 to 3 tablespoons beef mixture. Starting at stem end, roll up jelly-roll style, folding sides in as you go. Repeat with remaining cabbage rolls and beef mixture.

3. Place cabbage rolls seam side down and side by side in single layer in **CROCK-POT®** slow cooker. Pour in remaining ¾ cup tomato juice. Cover; cook on LOW 5 to 6 hours.

Sausage and Peppers over Polenta

Makes 4 servings

1 to 1½ pounds Italian sausage

2 bell peppers, sliced

1 medium onion, sliced

1 can (about 14 ounces) diced tomatoes with basil, oregano and garlic

1 tube (18 ounces) prepared polenta, cut into ½-inch-thick slices

1. Heat large skillet over medium heat. Add sausage; cook 8 minutes or until browned. Cut sausage into 1-inch pieces; remove to **CROCK-POT**® slow cooker. Stir in bell peppers, onion and tomatoes. Cover; cook on LOW 5½ to 6 hours or until vegetables are tender.

2. Preheat broiler. Spray large baking sheet with nonstick cooking spray.

3. Place polenta on prepared baking sheet. Broil 2 to 3 minutes on each side or until heated through and lightly browned. Serve polenta topped with sausage mixture.

Miso-Poached Salmon

Makes 6 servings

1½ cups water

2 green onions, cut into 2-inch-long pieces, plus additional for garnish

¼ cup yellow miso paste

¼ cup soy sauce

2 tablespoons sake

2 tablespoons mirin

1½ teaspoons grated fresh ginger

1 teaspoon minced garlic

6 (4 ounces *each*) salmon fillets

Hot cooked rice

1. Combine water, 2 green onions, miso paste, soy sauce, sake, mirin, ginger and garlic in **CROCK-POT®** slow cooker; stir to blend. Cover; cook on HIGH 30 minutes.

2. Turn **CROCK-POT®** slow cooker to LOW. Add salmon, skin side down. Cover; cook on LOW 30 minutes to 1 hour or until salmon turns opaque and flakes easily with fork. Serve over rice with cooking liquid. Garnish with additional green onions.

Chicken Meatballs in Spicy Tomato Sauce

Makes 4 servings

3 tablespoons olive oil, divided

1 medium onion, chopped

6 cloves garlic, minced

1½ teaspoons dried basil

¼ teaspoon red pepper flakes

2 cans (about 14 ounces *each*) diced tomatoes

3 tablespoons tomato paste

2 teaspoons salt, divided

1½ pounds ground chicken

2 egg yolks

1 teaspoon dried oregano

¼ teaspoon black pepper

Hot cooked pasta (optional)

1. Heat 2 tablespoons oil in large skillet over medium-high heat. Add onion, garlic, basil and red pepper flakes; cook and stir 5 minutes or until onion is softened. Remove half of mixture to **CROCK-POT®** slow cooker. Stir in diced tomatoes, tomato paste and 1 teaspoon salt.

2. Remove remaining onion mixture to large bowl. Add chicken, egg yolks, oregano, remaining 1 teaspoon salt and black pepper; mix well. Form mixture into 24 (1-inch) balls.

3. Heat remaining 1 tablespoon oil in large skillet. Add meatballs in batches; cook 7 minutes or until browned. Remove to **CROCK-POT®** slow cooker using slotted spoon. Cover; cook on LOW 4 to 5 hours. Serve over pasta, if desired.

Pot Roast with Bacon and Mushrooms

Makes 6 servings

6 slices bacon

1 (2½- to 3-pound) boneless beef chuck roast, trimmed

¾ teaspoon salt, divided

¼ teaspoon black pepper

¾ cup chopped shallots

8 ounces sliced white mushrooms

¼ ounce dried porcini mushrooms (optional)

4 cloves garlic, minced

1 teaspoon dried oregano

1 cup chicken broth

2 tablespoons tomato paste

Roasted Cauliflower (recipe follows, optional)

1. Heat large skillet over medium heat. Add bacon; cook 7 to 8 minutes until crisp-cooked and tender. Remove to large papertowel lined plate using slotted spoon; crumble.

2. Pour off all but 2 tablespoons fat from skillet. Season roast with ½ teaspoon salt and pepper. Heat skillet over medium-high heat. Add roast; cook 8 minutes or until well browned. Remove to large plate. Add shallots, white mushrooms, porcini mushrooms, if desired, garlic, oregano and remaining ¼ teaspoon salt; cook 3 to 4 minutes or until mushrooms are softened. Remove shallot mixture to **CROCK-POT**® slow cooker.

3. Stir bacon into **CROCK-POT**® slow cooker. Place roast on top of vegetables. Combine broth and tomato paste in small bowl; stir to blend. Pour broth mixture over roast. Cover; cook on LOW 8 hours. Prepare Roasted Cauliflower, if desired. Remove roast to large cutting board. Cover loosely with foil; let stand 10 minutes before slicing. Top each serving with vegetables and cooking liquid. Serve with Roasted Cauliflower, if desired.

Roasted Cauliflower: Preheat oven to 375°F. Break 1 head cauliflower into florets; coat with olive oil. Roast 20 minutes. Turn; roast 15 minutes. Makes 6 servings.

Couscous Stuffed Bell Peppers

Makes 4 servings

4 medium assorted color bell
    peppers

¾ cup plus ½ cup water, divided

½ teaspoon salt

⅔ cup uncooked couscous

8 ounces Mexican chorizo sausage,
    casings removed, cooked and
    crumbled

1 cup (4 ounces) shredded sharp
    Cheddar cheese, plus
    additional for topping

1 cup prepared corn and black
    bean salsa, divided

1. Cut top ¼ off each bell pepper. Remove and discard seeds. Finely dice tops of each bell pepper. Add diced peppers, ¾ cup water and salt to small saucepan; bring to a boil over high heat. Add couscous; cover and remove from heat. Let stand 5 minutes.

2. Remove couscous to large bowl. Add chorizo, 1 cup cheese and ½ cup salsa; mix well. Divide couscous mixture evenly among peppers.

3. Place ½ cup water in **CROCK-POT®** slow cooker. Place filled peppers in bottom. Cover; cook on LOW 4 to 5 hours or until filling is heated through and peppers are tender. Serve peppers topped with remaining ½ cup salsa and additional cheese, if desired.

Curried Cauliflower and Potatoes

Makes 4 to 6 servings

3 tablespoons vegetable oil

1 medium onion, chopped

1 tablespoon minced garlic

1 tablespoon curry powder

1½ teaspoons salt, plus additional
    for seasoning

1½ teaspoons grated fresh ginger

1 teaspoon ground turmeric

1 teaspoon yellow or brown
    mustard seeds

¼ teaspoon red pepper flakes

1 medium head cauliflower, cut
    into 1-inch pieces

2 pounds fingerling potatoes,
    cut into halves

½ cup water

1. Heat oil in medium skillet over medium heat. Add onion; cook 8 minutes or until softened. Add garlic, curry powder, 1½ teaspoons salt, ginger, turmeric, mustard seeds and red pepper flakes; cook and stir 1 minute. Remove onion mixture to **CROCK-POT®** slow cooker.

2. Stir in cauliflower, potatoes and water. Cover; cook on HIGH 4 hours. Season with additional salt, if desired.

BBQ Baked Beans

Makes 12 servings

3 cans (about 15 ounces *each*) white beans, drained

4 slices bacon, chopped

¾ cup prepared barbecue sauce

½ cup maple syrup

1½ teaspoons ground mustard

Coat inside of **CROCK-POT®** slow cooker with nonstick cooking spray. Add beans, bacon, barbecue sauce, syrup and mustard; stir to blend. Cover; cook on LOW 4 hours, stirring halfway through cooking time.

Brussels Sprouts with Bacon, Thyme and Raisins

Makes 8 servings

2 pounds Brussels sprouts

1 cup chicken broth

⅔ cup golden raisins

2 thick slices applewood smoked bacon, chopped

2 tablespoons chopped fresh thyme

Trim ends from sprouts; cut in half lengthwise through core (or in quarters). Combine sprouts, broth, raisins, bacon and thyme in **CROCK-POT®** slow cooker; stir to blend. Cover; cook on LOW 3 to 4 hours.

BBQ Baked Beans

Cheesy Polenta

Makes 6 servings

6 cups vegetable broth

1½ cups uncooked medium-grind instant polenta

½ cup grated Parmesan cheese, plus additional for serving

4 tablespoons unsalted butter, cubed

Fried sage leaves (optional)

1. Coat inside of **CROCK-POT**® slow cooker with nonstick cooking spray. Heat broth in large saucepan over high heat. Remove to **CROCK-POT**® slow cooker; whisk in polenta.

2. Cover; cook on LOW 2 to 2½ hours or until polenta is tender and creamy. Stir in ½ cup cheese and butter. Serve with additional cheese and garnish with sage leaves.

Red Cabbage and Apples

Makes 6 servings

1 small head red cabbage, cored and thinly sliced

1 large apple, peeled and grated

¾ cup sugar

½ cup red wine vinegar

1 teaspoon ground cloves

½ cup bacon, crisp-cooked and crumbled (optional)

Fresh apple slices (optional)

Combine cabbage, grated apple, sugar, vinegar and cloves in **CROCK-POT**® slow cooker; stir to blend. Cover; cook on HIGH 6 hours, stirring halfway through cooking time. Sprinkle with bacon, if desired. Garnish

Cheesy Polenta

Five-Ingredient Mushroom Stuffing

Makes 12 servings

6 tablespoons unsalted butter

2 medium onions, chopped

1 pound sliced white mushrooms

¼ teaspoon salt

5 cups bagged stuffing mix, any seasoning

1 cup vegetable broth

Fresh chopped Italian parsley

1. Melt butter in large skillet over medium-high heat. Add onions, mushrooms and salt; cook and stir 20 minutes or until vegetables are browned and most liquid is absorbed. Remove onion mixture to **CROCK-POT®** slow cooker.

2. Stir in stuffing mix and broth. Cover; cook on LOW 3 hours. Garnish with parsley.

Mashed Root Vegetables

Makes 6 servings

1 pound potatoes, peeled and cut into 1-inch pieces

1 pound turnips, peeled and cut into 1-inch pieces

12 ounces sweet potatoes, peeled and cut into 1-inch pieces

8 ounces parsnips, peeled and cut into ½-inch pieces

5 tablespoons butter

¼ cup water

2 teaspoons salt

¼ teaspoon black pepper

1 cup milk

1. Coat inside of **CROCK-POT®** slow cooker with nonstick cooking spray. Add potatoes, turnips, sweet potatoes, parsnips, butter, water, salt and pepper; stir to blend. Cover; cook on HIGH 3 to 4 hours.

2. Mash mixture with potato masher until smooth. Stir in milk. Cover; cook on HIGH 15 minutes.

Lemon and Tangerine Glazed Carrots

Makes 10 to 12 servings

6 cups sliced carrots

1½ cups apple juice

6 tablespoons butter

¼ cup packed brown sugar

2 tablespoons grated lemon peel

2 tablespoons grated tangerine peel

½ teaspoon salt

Chopped fresh Italian parsley (optional)

Combine carrots, apple juice, butter, brown sugar, lemon peel, tangerine peel and salt in **CROCK-POT®** slow cooker; stir to blend. Cover; cook on LOW 4 to 5 hours or on HIGH 1 to 3 hours. Garnish with parsley.

Gratin Potatoes with Asiago Cheese

Makes 4 to 6 servings

6 slices bacon, cut into 1-inch pieces

6 medium baking potatoes, thinly sliced

½ cup grated Asiago cheese

Salt and black pepper

1½ cups whipping cream

1. Heat large skillet over medium heat. Add bacon; cook and stir until crisp. Remove to paper towel-lined plate using slotted spoon.

2. Pour bacon drippings into **CROCK-POT®** slow cooker. Layer one fourth of potatoes on bottom of **CROCK-POT®** slow cooker. Sprinkle one fourth of bacon over potatoes and top with one fourth of cheese. Season with salt and pepper.

3. Repeat layers three times. Pour cream over all. Cover; cook on LOW 7 to 9 hours or on HIGH 5 to

Lemon and Tangerine Glazed Carrots

Slow-Cooked Succotash

Makes 8 servings

2 teaspoons olive oil

1 cup diced onion

1 cup diced green bell pepper

1 cup diced celery

1 teaspoon paprika

1½ cups frozen corn

1½ cups frozen lima beans

1 cup canned diced tomatoes

2 teaspoons dried parsley flakes
***or* 1 tablespoon minced fresh Italian parsley**

Salt and black pepper

1. Heat oil in large skillet over medium heat. Add onion, bell pepper and celery; cook and stir 5 minutes or until vegetables are crisp-tender. Stir in paprika.

2. Stir onion mixture, corn, beans, tomatoes, parsley flakes, salt and black pepper into **CROCK-POT®** slow cooker. Cover; cook on LOW 6 to 8 hours or on HIGH 3 to 4 hours.

Olive Oil Mashed Rutabagas

Makes 8 servings

1 (2½- to 3-pound) rutabaga
    (waxed turnip), peeled and cut
    into 1-inch pieces

4 cloves garlic

Boiling water

2 tablespoons olive oil

1 teaspoon salt

1 teaspoon dried thyme

1. Combine rutabaga, garlic and enough boiling water to cover by 1 inch in **CROCK-POT®** slow cooker. Cover; cook on LOW 7 to 8 hours.

2. Place rutabaga in food processor or blender; purée, adding water as necessary, to reach desired consistency. Stir in oil, salt and thyme.

Candied Sweet Potatoes

Makes 4 servings

3 medium sweet potatoes
    (1½ to 2 pounds), sliced into
    ½-inch rounds

½ cup water

¼ cup (½ stick) butter, cubed

2 tablespoons sugar

1 tablespoon vanilla

1 teaspoon ground nutmeg

Combine sweet potatoes, water, butter, sugar, vanilla and nutmeg in **CROCK-POT®** slow cooker; stir to blend. Cover; cook on LOW 7 hours or on HIGH 4 hours.

Olive Oil Mashed Rutabagas

Mashed Rutabagas and Potatoes

Makes 8 servings

2 pounds rutabagas, peeled and cut into ½-inch pieces

1 pound potatoes, peeled and cut into ½-inch pieces

½ cup milk

½ teaspoon ground nutmeg

2 tablespoons chopped fresh Italian parsley

Sprigs fresh Italian parsley (optional)

1. Place rutabagas and potatoes in **CROCK-POT®** slow cooker; add enough water to cover vegetables. Cover; cook on LOW 6 hours or on HIGH 3 hours. Remove vegetables to large bowl using slotted spoon. Discard cooking liquid.

2. Mash vegetables with potato masher. Add milk, nutmeg and chopped parsley; stir until smooth. Garnish with parsley sprigs.

Tarragon Carrots in White Wine

Makes 6 to 8 servings

8 medium carrots, cut into matchsticks

½ cup chicken broth

½ cup dry white wine

1 tablespoon lemon juice

1 tablespoon minced fresh tarragon

2 teaspoons finely chopped green onions

1½ teaspoons chopped fresh Italian parsley

1 clove garlic, minced

1 teaspoon salt

2 tablespoons melba toast, crushed

2 tablespoons cold water

1. Combine carrots, broth, wine, lemon juice, tarragon, green onions, parsley, garlic and salt in **CROCK-POT®** slow cooker; stir to blend. Cover; cook on LOW 2½ to 3 hours or on HIGH 1½ to 2 hours.

2. Dissolve toast crumbs in water in small bowl; add to carrots. Cover; cook on LOW 10 minutes or until thickened.

Poblano Creamed Corn

Makes 6 servings

4 whole poblano peppers

3 tablespoons olive oil

1 package (16 ounces) frozen corn

4 ounces cream cheese

3 slices American cheese

2 tablespoons butter

1½ tablespoons chicken broth

1 tablespoon chopped jalapeño pepper (optional)*

Salt and black pepper

*Jalapeño peppers can sting and irritate the skin, so wear rubber gloves when handling peppers and do not touch your eyes.

1. Preheat oven to 350°F. Spray large baking sheet with nonstick cooking spray. Place poblano peppers on prepared baking sheet; brush with oil. Bake 20 minutes or until outer skins loosen. When cool enough to handle, remove outer skin from 1 poblano pepper and mince. Cut remaining 3 poblano peppers in half and reserve.

2. Combine corn, cream cheese, American cheese, minced poblano peppers, butter, broth, jalapeño pepper, if desired, salt and black pepper in **CROCK-POT®** slow cooker. Cover; cook on LOW 4 to 5 hours. To serve, spoon corn into reserved poblano pepper halves.

A

Almonds: Overnight Breakfast Porridge, 10

Apple
Apple-Cinnamon Breakfast Risotto, 14
Lemon and Tangerine Glazed Carrots, 112
Red Cabbage and Apples, 106
Spiced Vanilla Applesauce, 22
Apple-Cinnamon Breakfast Risotto, 14
Apricot: Lamb and Chickpea Stew, 70

B

Bacon
BBQ Baked Beans, 104
Beef and Beet Borscht, 58
Brussels Sprouts with Bacon, Thyme and Raisins, 104
Gratin Potatoes with Asiago Cheese, 112
Maple, Bacon and Raspberry Pancake, 8
Pot Roast with Bacon and Mushrooms, 98
Bananas: Blueberry-Banana Pancakes, 20
Barbecue: BBQ Baked Beans, 104
BBQ Baked Beans, 104
Beans, Black
Black Bean, Zucchini and Corn Enchiladas, 32
Three-Bean Chili with Chorizo, 56
Beans, Cannellini: Vegetable-Bean Pasta Sauce, 40
Beans, Green
Chickpea and Vegetable Curry, 34
Thai Red Curry with Tofu, 44
Beans, Kidney
Corn Bread and Bean Casserole, 48
Three-Bean Chili with Chorizo, 56
Beans, Lima: Slow-Cooked Succotash, 114
Beans, Navy: White Chicken Chili, 76
Beans, Pinto
Corn Bread and Bean Casserole, 48
Three-Bean Chili with Chorizo, 56
Beans, White: BBQ Baked Beans, 104

Beef *(see also* Beef, Ground*)*
Beef and Beet Borscht, 58
Beef and Quinoa Stuffed Cabbage Rolls, 90
Braised Short Ribs with Aromatic Spices, 78
Easy Beef Stew, 62
Pot Roast with Bacon and Mushrooms, 98
Texas Chili, 74
Beef and Beet Borscht, 58
Beef and Quinoa Stuffed Cabbage Rolls, 90
Beef, Ground: Easy Salisbury Steak, 80
Beets: Beef and Beet Borscht, 58
Berry
Blueberry-Banana Pancakes, 20
Maple, Bacon and Raspberry Pancake, 8
Overnight Breakfast Porridge, 10
Black Bean, Zucchini and Corn Enchiladas, 32
Blueberry-Banana Pancakes, 20
Braised Short Ribs with Aromatic Spices, 78
Broccoli: Broccoli Cheddar Soup, 72
Broccoli Cheddar Soup, 72
Brussels Sprouts with Bacon, Thyme and Raisins, 104

C

Cabbage
Beef and Beet Borscht, 58
Beef and Quinoa Stuffed Cabbage Rolls, 90
Red Cabbage and Apples, 106
Candied Sweet Potatoes, 116
Carrots
Beef and Beet Borscht, 58
Chicken and Mushroom Stew, 66
Chicken and Vegetable Soup, 54
Chickpea and Vegetable Curry, 34
Easy Beef Stew, 62
Lemon and Tangerine Glazed Carrots, 112
Tarragon Carrots in White Wine, 120
Vegetable-Bean Pasta Sauce, 40

Cauliflower
Curried Cauliflower and Potatoes, 102
Roasted Cauliflower, 98
Cheesy Polenta, 106
Chicken
Chicken and Mushroom Stew, 66
Chicken and Vegetable Soup, 54
Chicken Meatballs in Spicy Tomato Sauce, 96
Hash Brown and Sausage Breakfast Casserole, 24
Pineapple and Butternut Squash Braised Chicken, 86
White Chicken Chili, 76
Chicken and Mushroom Stew, 66
Chicken and Vegetable Soup, 54
Chicken Meatballs in Spicy Tomato Sauce, 96
Chickpea and Vegetable Curry, 34
Chickpeas
Chickpea and Vegetable Curry, 34
Lamb and Chickpea Stew, 70
Corn
Black Bean, Zucchini and Corn Enchiladas, 32
Corn Bread and Bean Casserole, 48
Poblano Creamed Corn, 122
Slow-Cooked Succotash, 114
Corn Bread and Bean Casserole, 48
Couscous Stuffed Bell Peppers, 100
Curried Cauliflower and Potatoes, 102

E
Easy Beef Stew, 62
Easy Salisbury Steak, 80
Eggplant
Eggplant Parmesan, 38
Italian Eggplant with Millet and Pepper Stuffing, 42
Thai Red Curry with Tofu, 44
Ziti Ratatouille, 50
Eggplant Parmesan, 38

Eggs
Hash Brown and Sausage Breakfast Casserole, 24
Mediterranean Frittata, 28
Savory Sausage Bread Pudding, 16
Wake-Up Potato and Sausage Breakfast Casserole, 12

F
Farro Risotto with Mushrooms and Spinach, 30
Five-Ingredient Mushroom Stuffing, 108

G
Gratin Potatoes with Asiago Cheese, 112

H
Hash Brown and Sausage Breakfast Casserole, 24
Hominy: Pozole Rojo, 68
Honey: Pulled Pork with Honey-Chipotle Barbecue Sauce, 88

I
Italian Eggplant with Millet and Pepper Stuffing, 42

L
Lamb and Chickpea Stew, 70
Lamb: Lamb and Chickpea Stew, 70
Leeks: Chicken and Mushroom Stew, 66
Lemon and Tangerine Glazed Carrots, 112

M
Maple, Bacon and Raspberry Pancake, 8
Maple-Dry Rubbed Ribs, 84
Mashed Root Vegetables, 110
Mashed Rutabagas and Potatoes, 118
Mediterranean Frittata, 28
Millet: Italian Eggplant with Millet and Pepper Stuffing, 42

Miso-Poached Salmon, 94
Mushroom
Chicken and Mushroom Stew, 66
Easy Salisbury Steak, 80
Farro Risotto with Mushrooms and Spinach, 30
Five-Ingredient Mushroom Stuffing, 108
Hash Brown and Sausage Breakfast Casserole, 24
Mediterranean Frittata, 28
Pot Roast with Bacon and Mushrooms, 98
Vegetable-Bean Pasta Sauce, 40

N

No-Fuss Macaroni and Cheese, 52

O

Oats
Overnight Breakfast Porridge, 10
Raisin-Oat Quick Bread, 26
Okra: Shrimp and Okra Gumbo, 64
Olive Oil Mashed Rutabagas, 116
Olives
Mediterranean Frittata, 28
Ziti Ratatouille, 50
Orange Date-Nut Bread, 18
Overnight Breakfast Porridge, 10

P

Pasta
Chickpea and Vegetable Curry, 34
Couscous Stuffed Bell Peppers, 100
No-Fuss Macaroni and Cheese, 52
Summer Squash Lasagna, 46
Vegetable-Bean Pasta Sauce, 40
Ziti Ratatouille, 50
Pecans: Orange Date-Nut Bread, 18
Pineapple and Butternut Squash Braised Chicken, 86

Poblano Creamed Corn, 122
Polenta
Cheesy Polenta, 106
Sausage and Peppers over Polenta, 92
Pork
Couscous Stuffed Bell Peppers, 100
Maple-Dry Rubbed Ribs, 84
Pozole Rojo, 68
Pulled Pork with Honey-Chipotle Barbecue Sauce, 88
Sausage and Peppers over Polenta, 92
Savory Sausage Bread Pudding, 16
Shrimp and Okra Gumbo, 64
Shrimp Jambalaya, 82
Three-Bean Chili with Chorizo, 56
Wake-Up Potato and Sausage Breakfast Casserole, 12
Potatoes *(see also* Potatoes, Sweet*)*
Broccoli Cheddar Soup, 72
Curried Cauliflower and Potatoes, 102
Easy Beef Stew, 62
Gratin Potatoes with Asiago Cheese, 112
Hash Brown and Sausage Breakfast Casserole, 24
Mashed Root Vegetables, 110
Mashed Rutabagas and Potatoes, 118
Wake-Up Potato and Sausage Breakfast Casserole, 12
Potatoes, Sweet
Braised Short Ribs with Aromatic Spices, 78
Candied Sweet Potatoes, 116
Mashed Root Vegetables, 110
Thai Red Curry with Tofu, 44
Pot Roast with Bacon and Mushrooms, 98
Pozole Rojo, 68
Pulled Pork with Honey-Chipotle Barbecue Sauce, 88

Q

Quinoa
Beef and Quinoa Stuffed Cabbage Rolls, 90
Overnight Breakfast Porridge, 10

R

Raisins and Dates

Brussels Sprouts with Bacon, Thyme and Raisins, 104

Chickpea and Vegetable Curry, 34

Orange Date-Nut Bread, 18

Overnight Breakfast Porridge, 10

Raisin-Oat Quick Bread, 26

Raisin-Oat Quick Bread, 26

Red Cabbage and Apples, 106

Rice

Apple-Cinnamon Breakfast Risotto, 14

Shrimp Jambalaya, 82

Risotto: Farro Risotto with Mushrooms and Spinach, 30

Roasted Cauliflower, 98

Rutabagas

Mashed Rutabagas and Potatoes, 118

Olive Oil Mashed Rutabagas, 116

S

Salmon: Miso-Poached Salmon, 94

Salsa

Black Bean, Zucchini and Corn Enchiladas, 32

Couscous Stuffed Bell Peppers, 100

Sausage and Peppers over Polenta, 92

Savory Sausage Bread Pudding, 16

Shrimp

Shrimp and Okra Gumbo, 64

Shrimp Jambalaya, 82

Shrimp and Okra Gumbo, 64

Shrimp Jambalaya, 82

Slow-Cooked Succotash, 114

Spiced Vanilla Applesauce, 22

Spinach

Farro Risotto with Mushrooms and Spinach, 30

Hash Brown and Sausage Breakfast Casserole, 24

Mediterranean Frittata, 28

Squash

Pineapple and Butternut Squash Braised Chicken, 86

Summer Squash Lasagna, 46

Summer Squash Lasagna, 46

T

Tarragon Carrots in White Wine, 120

Texas Chili, 74

Thai Red Curry with Tofu, 44

Three-Bean Chili with Chorizo, 56

Tofu

Thai Red Curry with Tofu, 44

Tofu Tikka Masala, 36

Tofu Tikka Masala, 36

Turkey: Turkey Chili, 60

Turkey Chili, 60

V

Vegetable-Bean Pasta Sauce, 40

W

Wake-Up Potato and Sausage Breakfast Casserole, 12

White Chicken Chili, 76

Wine

Chicken and Mushroom Stew, 66

Tarragon Carrots in White Wine, 120

Z

Ziti Ratatouille, 50

Zucchini

Black Bean, Zucchini and Corn Enchiladas, 32

Summer Squash Lasagna, 46

Ziti Ratatouille, 50

VOLUME MEASUREMENTS (dry)

$^1/_8$ teaspoon = 0.5 mL
$^1/_4$ teaspoon = 1 mL
$^1/_2$ teaspoon = 2 mL
$^3/_4$ teaspoon = 4 mL
1 teaspoon = 5 mL
1 tablespoon = 15 mL
2 tablespoons = 30 mL
$^1/_4$ cup = 60 mL
$^1/_3$ cup = 75 mL
$^1/_2$ cup = 125 mL
$^2/_3$ cup = 150 mL
$^3/_4$ cup = 175 mL
1 cup = 250 mL
2 cups = 1 pint = 500 mL
3 cups = 750 mL
4 cups = 1 quart = 1 L

VOLUME MEASUREMENTS (fluid)

1 fluid ounce (2 tablespoons) = 30 mL
4 fluid ounces ($^1/_2$ cup) = 125 mL
8 fluid ounces (1 cup) = 250 mL
12 fluid ounces (1$^1/_2$ cups) = 375 mL
16 fluid ounces (2 cups) = 500 mL

WEIGHTS (mass)

$^1/_2$ ounce = 15 g
1 ounce = 30 g
3 ounces = 90 g
4 ounces = 120 g
8 ounces = 225 g
10 ounces = 285 g
12 ounces = 360 g
16 ounces = 1 pound = 450 g

DIMENSIONS

$^1/_{16}$ inch = 2 mm
$^1/_8$ inch = 3 mm
$^1/_4$ inch = 6 mm
$^1/_2$ inch = 1.5 cm
$^3/_4$ inch = 2 cm
1 inch = 2.5 cm

OVEN TEMPERATURES

250°F = 120°C
275°F = 140°C
300°F = 150°C
325°F = 160°C
350°F = 180°C
375°F = 190°C
400°F = 200°C
425°F = 220°C
450°F = 230°C

BAKING PAN SIZES

Utensil	Size in Inches/Quarts	Metric Volume	Size in Centimeters
Baking or Cake Pan (square or rectangular)	8×8×2	2 L	20×20×5
	9×9×2	2.5 L	23×23×5
	12×8×2	3 L	30×20×5
	13×9×2	3.5 L	33×23×5
Loaf Pan	8×4×3	1.5 L	20×10×7
	9×5×3	2 L	23×13×7
Round Layer Cake Pan	8×1½	1.2 L	20×4
	9×1½	1.5 L	23×4
Pie Plate	8×1¼	750 mL	20×3
	9×1¼	1 L	23×3
Baking Dish or Casserole	1 quart	1 L	—
	1½ quart	1.5 L	—
	2 quart	2 L	—